1964
Railways &
Recollections

Contents

Series Introduction

Welcome to a brand new and innovative series!

Railway publishing has been around almost as long as the railways themselves and there have been countless books with a historical theme, telling the story of a particular line, say, and occasionally linking the subject to its social context, but never before has there been, in such an accessible way, a juxtapositioning of photographic illustration of a railway subject with the events, happenings and highlights of a wider sphere and calendar. This series will, initially, take a particular year and place the views displayed alongside a carefully selected pot-pourri of what happened in that twelve-month period. The vast majority of the images in the first few books are from the Ray Ruffell collection, held by the publisher, but material from other sources will be interspersed where felt necessary to maintain appropriate variety. Ray was a railwayman and photographer of equal merit and the main criterion for inclusion in these books is for the images to be both interesting and aesthetically pleasing within a chosen theme.

The books are aimed at a more general market than mere railway aficionados or enthusiasts and the authors hope and trust that they will be sure in their aim and that you, the reader, will find much to enjoy, appreciate, enthuse about and even smile about! And it is hoped that some of your own memories are stirred along the way and that you may wish to share these with friends!

First published in 2006
ISBN 1 85794 275 2   ISBN 978 1 85794 275 0

Silver Link Publishing Ltd
The Trundle
Ringstead Road
Great Addington
Kettering
Northants NN14 4BW

Tel/Fax: 01536 330588
email: sales@nostalgiacollection.com
Website: www.nostalgiacollection.com

British Library Cataloguing in Publication Data
A catalogue record for this book is available from the British Library.
Printed and bound in Great Britain

Above **SANDHURST** Once a common sight throughout the country, colour light signals were rapidly replacing traditional semaphores by this time. Happily, on 8 March, this Down Advance signal, with its delightful lattice post, still points skywards to allow 'Standard 4' 2-6-4T No. 80032 to pull away from Sandhurst and proceed with the 3.35 p.m. (Sundays-only) Redhill-Reading passenger service.

Frontispiece **WATERLOO** Dieselisation and electrification had been making massive inroads to our traditional railway operations in the two decades prior to 1964, but steam still clung on in most parts, although often fighting a rearguard action! Empty stock workings and the like at London's various termini were a case in point and, on 4 July, W Class 2-6-4T No. 31914 makes a spirited exit from Waterloo with a rake of vans holding empty milk tanks. The loco was withdrawn just two months later.

Introduction
Railways & Recollections 1964

As with any year, 1964 was a mixture of good and bad, important and trivial (in some eyes!), world events, political and social change and, on the UK's railways, a continuation of great upheaval following the twin prongs of the 1955 Modernisation Plan – and the introduction of dieselisation – and the Beeching Plan – to close many hundreds of miles of our railway system.

A potentially explosive incident took place between the USA and North Korea in the Gulf of Tonkin; China exploded her first atomic bomb; Nelson Mandela was imprisoned in South Africa for opposing Apartheid; and, in America, the Surgeon General warned against the dangers of cigarette smoking! In the UK, The Beatles were still 'on the up', with their memorable trips to the USA, Australia and New Zealand; and, on the roads, the first Ford Mustang was produced. January 3rd saw the 72nd birthday of J R R Tolkien, whose books The Hobbit and Lord of the Rings were just beginning to gather cult reading status amongst University students, having been largely ignored since their publication many years earlier. July 21st was the 18th birthday of Cat Stevens,

later to become a hit singer/songwriter before converting to Islam; and August 3rd was the 21st birthday of one of your authors!

Musically, the year started with The Dave Clark Five feeling Glad All Over at No.2 in the Charts and ended with The Beatles' appropriately titled I Feel Fine racing to become the sixth in their incredible run of eleven consecutive No.1 hits! In between, there were No.1's for The Bachelors (Diane), The Four Pennies (Juliet), The Animals (The House of the Rising Sun), The Rolling Stones (It's All Over Now), and Roy Orbison (Oh, Pretty Woman). Radio Caroline launched their broadcasting challenge to the BBC at Easter, out on the ocean waves, with The Rolling Stones' Not Fade Away; the Olympic Games took place in Tokyo; Mods and Rockers 'enjoyed' their skirmishes at various seaside resorts; My Fair Lady and Mary Poppins took the lion's share of the Oscars; and at Wembley on 14th May, West Ham United beat Preston North End 3-2 in the F A Cup.

On the railways, line closures that had slightly accelerated during 1963, literally went into overdrive this following year, with no fewer than 362 services, lines or parts of lines ended – virtually one per day for the whole year! Among these were the closure of the ex-M&SWJR route between Swindon Town and Cirencester Watermoor on (appropriately) April Fool's Day (!); withdrawal of passenger services over the two branches from Kemble five days later; passengers between Northampton (Castle) and Peterborough (East); closure of ex-LNW Seaton to Uppingham and ex-GNR Humberstone-Melton Mowbray North routes; passengers from Barry (Town) to Bridgend; closure between Caernarfon-Llanberis; and the ex-DN&SR 'cross-country' route from Didcot to Newbury. Readers will no doubt have their own 'favourites'!

Your authors hope you enjoy the mix and will, like Oliver, come back for more!

John Stretton
Oxfordshire

Peter Townsend
Northamptonshire

April 2006

Background **GUILDFORD** Working on shed was not just about driving or servicing the locos, it often meant hard manual labour. On Guildford shed, two fitters slowly roll a wheelset for the Q1 loco beyond towards its destination.

1964
Happenings (1)

JANUARY

- Leyland Motors announce supply of 450 buses to Cuba
- Pope Paul VI visits Jerusalem
- John Glenn enters politics
- France & China establish diplomatic relations

FEBRUARY

- The Beatles visit New York and appear on the Ed Sullivan Show
- The Leaning Tower of Pisa in danger of falling Italian Government launches appeal for help to stabilize the structure

MARCH

- Malta gains independence
- Coronation of King Constantine II of Greece
- Ford of America build the first Mustang

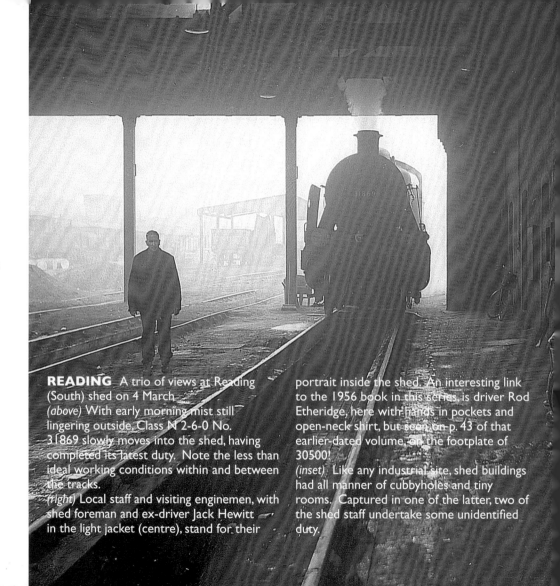

READING A trio of views at Reading (South) shed on 4 March
(above) With early morning mist still lingering outside, Class N 2-6-0 No. 31869 slowly moves into the shed, having completed its latest duty. Note the less than ideal working conditions within and between the tracks.
(right) Local staff and visiting enginemen, with shed foreman and ex-driver Jack Hewitt in the light jacket (centre), stand for their portrait inside the shed. An interesting link to the 1956 book in this series, is driver Rod Etheridge, here with hands in pockets and open-neck shirt, but seen on p. 43 of that earlier-dated volume, on the footplate of 30500!
(inset) Like any industrial site, shed buildings had all manner of cubbyholes and tiny rooms. Captured in one of the latter, two of the shed staff undertake some unidentified duty.

1964
The Steam Locomotive Shed
still a hive of activity!

Left **READING** A hacksaw in hand, two of the shed staff work on some item gripped tightly in the vice.

Below left The Enginemen's Cabin! What used to be a storeroom at Reading (South) shed has been converted for staff accommodation but, especially by today's standards, it is still somewhat 'rough and ready'. Two cleaners pause for their portrait during their card game, while beyond are (standing) a fireman and two shed staff and (seated) three drivers. The date is 4 March and one wonders whether the rather Heath Robinson-ish stove in the centre of the room is in active service. Note the proliferation of lockers around the walls.

Below right Another view of shed foreman Jack Hewitt, this time seated at his desk, in his 'domain'. Woe betide any staff members called to the room for a dressing down! Note the fine collection of phones - the telecoms revolution is limited to the more modern shape of phone to the right on Jack's desk. Strange that replicas of the phone on the left are now sold at a premium!

Below **READING** More ash, clinker and the odd lump of coal litter the ground as Driver Vic Woodham, oil can in hand, follows his pre-duty routine maintenance. His charge, U Class 2-6-0 No.31790 stands temporarily idle on Reading (South) shed before moving to the town's Southern station, to operate the 12.05 p.m. passenger service to Tonbridge.

READING Reading (South) was a relatively small shed, but, as can be seen from the collection of photographs in this volume, the number of staff employed and the jobs they undertook are far more than might have been imagined. On 4 March again, fitter Frank Burrows is Lord of all he surveys, including wooden lockers, stove and a variety of implements.

READING From the mid-1950s onwards, it became increasingly difficult for the railways to recruit staff. Partly this was because the career path for staff – engine drivers especially – was long and drawn out but, also, 'white collar' jobs were increasingly popular and available and the dirt of the railways, particularly when dealing with steam, just did not appeal. Cleaning out locomotives was a dirty and thankless task and both the piles of ash and clinker either side of the pit at Reading (South) shed on 4 March and the expression on this gentleman's face say it all!

a common feature throughout the UK. The Class was introduced in 1946, in LMS days, whereas 41287 was not delivered until 2 December 1950 (to Crewe North shed) and, thus, was a BR asset. Transfer to the SR at Brighton came in 1961, and the loco here wears the appropriate 75A shedplate. Transfer to Guildford came two months after this view, followed by a move to Basingstoke a year later, from where the end came on 22 August 1966.

Below **READING** Back at Reading (South), two more railway servants are captured for posterity, this time enjoying a 'char' in the rest room.

GUILDFORD Outside on 8 March at Guildford, Ivatt Class 2 2-6-2T – known throughout the system as 'Mickey Mouse' – No. 41287 stands on the turntable immediately outside the shed building. While running tender or tank first was generally not a great problem, both authorities and crew alike certainly preferred 'boiler first'. To achieve this, locos often had to be turned and turntables such as the one here were

Left **GUILDFORD** Modern railways are complicated to operate, especially the motive power, with its proliferation of computers and electronics. In comparison, it could be thought that the steam engine was a very simple affair, but this view of the cab of SR Q1 0-6-0 No.33035 belies this assumption.

Seen while under repair on Guildford shed on 26 February, the footplate of the engine shows that there was more to operating a steam locomotive than perhaps meets the eye, with valves, levers, gauges and piping all performing specific functions. Introduced in 1942, to Oliver Bullied's 'Austerity' design, the principle here was for cheap, sturdy locomotives that were less troublesome to service than many types that had gone before.

Previously allocated to Tonbridge shed, it was transferred to Guildford on 26 May 1961 and withdrawn from there four days short of four months after this view.

Right **GUILDFORD** Not a mirror image of that seen on p.10, but a view of Q1 No.33035, under repair, from the opposite side. Note the boards from the footplate temporarily stored inside the side cabsheet!

1964

Happenings (2)

MARCH

- Jack Ruby found guilty of murdering Lee Harvey Oswald - assasin of President John F. Kennedy

- European Space Agency established.

- Anchorage (USA) and surrounding area suffer from major earthquake over 100 killed.

- Radio Caroline (North) starts Pirate Radio transmission from ship anchored off Ramsey Isle of Man

GUILDFORD Our final look at the engine shed in this section again shows the appeal for the enthusiast, with a healthy collection of locos all in one place, but, also, the downside from the operators point of view – arranging for locomotives to be serviced and in the right order to be released for their next duties and the disposal of the steam locomotives' waste products! Seen from the station footbridge, the collection includes 'Standard 5s', Q1s, Us and Ns, with Nos. 31790, 33001 and 34014 *Budleigh Salterton* identified by the photographer.

1964
The Hampshire Hog
Another line killed by the axe!

Left **HAMPSTEAD NORRIS** On 14 March, the Railway Enthusiasts' Club ran its 'The Hampshire Hog' railtour, from Ash to Didcot, out via Eastleigh, Winchester and Newbury and returning by way of Reading, Staines Central and Farnborough.

A SR M7 0-4-4T should have hauled the trip from Eastleigh, but the locomotive sent from Salisbury for this purpose failed at Eastleigh and, consequently, Ivatt's Class 2 'Mickey Mouse' 2-6-2T No. 41329 took over.

It is here at the other end of the train, as the tour pauses on the outward leg at Hampstead Norris station on the Didcot, Newbury & Southampton Railway route (colloquially known as the 'Dirty, Noisy and Slow' line!). The tour was graced with typical dull, wet March weather and the young boy, left, almost seems driven to want to end it all!

The line had closed to passengers on 10 September 1962 and would close completely five months after this view.

Many older enthusiasts will no doubt recall that City class 4-4-0 No 3440 *City of Truro* was a regularly rostered loco on service trains on this route, following its restoration to the main line during 1957. This was, reputedly, the first steam locomotive to exceed 100 mph - a speed it was unlikely to achieve on the DN&SR!

HAMPSTEAD NORRIS We return to Hampstead Norris – see p.14 – and have walked to the opposite end of the train. The rain has either bated or stopped, as some of the tour participants are leisurely inspecting both station and locomotive.

The father and son (?) standing between the rails could be in danger, if the signal at the far end of the platform is to be believed. It appears to show that a train is expected! Interestingly, the railway again seems to have had its own idea as to spelling, as the local village was actually Hampstead Norreys! At the time of writing, the village is home to 'The Living Rainforest', housed in two large conservatories, containing exotic plants, free-flying birds and butterflies, as well as some animals.

Railtours have long been popular with enthusiasts and, on occasions, they even provided the unexpected. In dull, damp and dismal late-winter conditions the persistent rain enlivens the view of ex-LSWR M7 0-4-4T No. 30667, intensifying the effect of wreathing it in escaping steam as it reverses out of the station with a short rake of empty stock. On the opposite platform, the assembled throng have raincoats on and collars up as they huddle under the awning. One wonders if any were wishing their model railway could recreate the steam effects! Presumably the M7 was suffering more leakages than were healthy, as it was withdrawn in May of this year.

1964
Happenings (3)

APRIL

- The Beatles take the top 5 slots in the Billboard Singles chart!
- Ford of America unveil the Mustang to the Public - the legend begins!
- BBC 2 launched on 20 April
- Tanzania formed as Tanganyika and Zanzibar merge

MAY

- Habitat launched by Terrance Conran
- Over 300 killed and over 480 injured as football fans riot at Peru versus Argentina match in Lima

JUNE

- Nelson Mandela jailed after receiving a life sentence from South Afrcan court
- US Senator Edward Kennedy suffers serious injuries in plane crash, in which the pilot is killed

'THE HAMPSHIRE HOG' railtour of 14 March set out from Ash station behind Q1 0-6-0 No. 33035. The route hauled by this loco included Aldershot, Alton, Alresford, and Winchester City before its arrival at Eastleigh and the replacement by 'Mickey Mouse' 41329 already seen at Hampstead Norris.

The rain was incessant on this early stage of the tour and evidence of the downpour, as the train pulls into the platform, can be judged by the umbrellas, the behaviour of some out in the open and the raindrops actually being visible in this photograph!

Note the car on the platform! Note also that our tour loco is the very same one that was seen inside Guildford shed on 26 February – pp.10 and 11!

1964 was the year in which the 'Beeching Report' really began to bite with over 1000 miles of track being closed during the year. The running of rail tours gathered pace and the day of 'the last train' became a strange mix - passengers would turn up in such numbers that extra carriages were needed, brass bands, bunting and film crews were very often on hand and rather than a sad affair they could take on an eerie air of celebration!

BRITISH RAILWAYS BOARD

The Reshaping of British Railways

PART 1: REPORT

LONDON
HER MAJESTY'S STATIONERY OFFICE

1964
The train now approaching platform...

SANDHURST Probably the first thing that comes to mind at the mention of Sandhurst is the prestigious Royal Military Academy, formed in 1947 from the merger of older organisations at Woolwich (1741) and Camberley (1800).

The town is full of history, however and dates back to at least 1316, when it belonged to the Bishop of Salisbury. In much later times it was placed on the railway map when the South Eastern & Chatham Railway built a branch between Ash and Reading, well away from its normal sphere of influence!

Sandhurst Halt is here covered in snow, as seen around 7.05 a.m. on 16 March.
N Class 2-6-0 No. 31869 slows for the brief stop as the 6.35 a.m. from Guildford, to pick up the small handful of passengers bound for Reading. It bears headcode discs denoting the Redhill-Reading route and with the right-hand one proclaiming duty no 163.

1964
The train now standing at platform...

SANDHURST Another view of the diminutive Sandhurst Halt, in more pleasant climes but, perhaps surprisingly, eight days prior to the view on the previous page!

This is Sunday, 8 March and again the train is heading for Reading, this time as the 3.35 p.m. (Sundays-only) from Redhill. 'Standard 4' 2-6-4T No. 80032 was new in 1952 and allocated to Brighton. It moved to Redhill on 6 January 1964 and here bears the appropriate '75B' shedplate on the smokebox door.

It moved to Bournemouth in June 1965 and was withdrawn from there on 20 February 1967, after only 15 years life!

This type of locomotive, introduced in 1951, was one included in Hornby-Dublo's catalogue and both of your authors inherited No. 80054 with their first train sets!

Left **SLINFOLD** Situated on the ex-LB&SCR branch from Christ's Hospital to Peasmarsh Junction, just south of Guildford, Slinfold was not a station that was often photographed. We have a rare sight, therefore, on 22 February as the 8.04 a.m. Guildford-Horsham stopper pauses for any joining or embarking passengers and for its portrait to be taken. Keeping a watchful eye on affairs on the platform are Guard C. Jeal and the station porter.

Snapped on a dull morning using a shutter speed of 1/50th of a second and aperture f5.6, yet another 'Mickey Mouse', No. 41325, is near the end of its short run, but wearing a headcode as a mixture of disc and lamp! The branch closed to passengers a little over a year after this view, on 14 June 1965.

1964 Arrivals

Nicolas Cage	*actor*	7 January
Bridget Fonda	*actress*	27 January
Christopher Eccleston	*actor*	16 February
Matt Dillon	*actor*	18 February
Juliette Binoche	*actress*	9 March
Prince Edward		10 March
Shane Richie	*actor*	10 March
Martin Donnelly	*racing driver*	26 March
Russell Crowe	*actor*	7 April
Adrian Moorhouse	*swimmer*	24 May
Kathy Burke	*actress/comedienne*	13 June
Johnny Herbert	*racingdriver*	25 June
Bonnie Langford	*actress*	22 July
Sandra Bullock	*actress*	26 July
Jim Corr	*singer/musician*	31 July
Keanu Reeves	*actor*	2 September

1964
The train now departing from platform...

Above **GUILDFORD** At least in steam days you knew which way trains were travelling! On 28 February, 'Standard 4' 2-6-0 No. 76032 exudes plenty of white exhaust as it accelerates away from Guildford station with the 12.05 p.m. Reading-Tonbridge service. The signalman watches from the balcony of his box, as the train passes, while a ganger casually inspects some item on the ground. The engine shed can just be glimpsed to the right. Note the variety of Southern coaching stock and the vans immediately behind the loco.

Right **SANDHURST** We briefly return to the very wintry conditions at Sandhurst Halt on 16 March, to witness the 6.35 a.m. Guildford-Reading service continue on its way, leaving a powdery snow trail behind it. N Class 2-6-0 No. 31869 thankfully seems to have plenty of steam available.

The winter of 1963/64 was by no means as harsh as that of the previous year. The railways proved their worth as roads were buried in drifts in excess of 20 feet deep in many parts. The railways of course suffered from delays and blocked lines but were generally up and running well before the snow ploughs managed to clear the roads - particularly to more isolated towns and villages. Finding the road could in itself present a problem, whereas the rails provided a clear course to navigate!

Opposite **WATERLOO** Steam finished on the Southern Region in the summer of 1967, so, on this day – 12 May – a very smart-looking 'Merchant Navy' 4-6-2 No. 35024 *East Asiatic Company* has a few more years to operate front line services.

With Driver Burton of Salisbury and his fireman at the helm and leaning out for their portrait, the train eases out of Waterloo station with the 'down' 'Atlantic Coast Express', bound for the Devon coast, without the usual headboard on this occasion. Note the wooden boarding protecting the 'live rail' that provides current to the electric multiple units using the station.

1964
Waterloo sunset?
Not quite for steam...

Above **WATERLOO** With Waterloo being such a huge station, with a myriad of tracks leading in and out, there were often simultaneous departures on adjacent tracks and it was not unusual for there to be a 'race' between two trains. On 26 March, it looks as though the steam departure is determined to outrun the electric service to its right, with 'Merchant Navy' 4-6-2 No. 35008 *Orient Line* putting up a smoke shield to 'blind' the electric's driver! With plenty of exhaust, as *Orient Line* lifts the heavy 'down' (i.e. away from London) 'Bournemouth Belle' Pullman away from the station, the Waterloo-Guildford via Epsom electric service (code 16) has little chance of overtaking.

WATERLOO On the same day, but now in fading light, yet another 'Merchant Navy' begins a long run westwards from this London terminus. With steam to spare, apparently, No. 35023 *Holland-Afrika Line* eases out of the platform with the 6 p.m. express bound for Exeter, passing 'lookalike' 'West Country' 4-6-2 34096 *Trevone*.

1964 Departures				
Alan Ladd,	actor	(b. 1913)	29 January
Peter Lorre	actor	(b. 1904)	23 March
Jawaharlal Nehru	PM of India	(b. 1889)	27 May
Jim Reeves	singer	(b. 1923)	31 July
Sean O'Casey	writer	(b. 1880)	18 September
Harpo Marx	comedian	(b. 1888)	28 September
Cole Porter	composer	(b. 1891)	15 October
Herbert Hoover	31st US President	(b. 1874)	29 October
Sam Cooke	singer	(b. 1931)	11 December

Left **WATERLOO** On p.1 we saw W Class 2-6-4T shunting empty stock at Waterloo on 4 July. Here we have the same locomotive three months earlier, on Sunday, 5 April and still on empty stock movements. In this view, it stands at the station's buffer stops, having brought in the stock from Clapham Junction to work the 10.30 a.m. express to Bournemouth and Weymouth. As seen earlier, its useful life was not to last for much longer, with withdrawal, from Feltham shed, in September. Note the water column standing ready to quench the thirst of arriving steam locomotives; and the sign for 'BOAC', as 'British Airways' was then known.

Right **HAWES** A change of scenery takes us to Hawes, at the end of the long ex-NER branch from Northallerton. The date is 25 April and B16/2 4-6-0 No. 61435 has reached 'the end', mid-way through the RCTS 'The North Yorkshireman' railtour. Passenger services on the branch had ceased ten years earlier on 26 April 1954, with complete closure to this out of the way spot from Redmire, two-thirds of the way from Northallerton, just two days after this tour! This train was historic in being the very last passenger service along the branch. The tour suffered from being over ambitious – leading to pathing problems from unrealistic scheduling – slow running due to indifferent track conditions and, to cap it all, bucketfuls of Yorkshire rain! Note the 'smart' clothes of the day and almost exclusively the wearing of ties!

1964
Catch it while you can!
North Yorkshire farewell tour

Opposite **HAWES** The Yorkshire weather is still dull but, at least, the rain appears to be holding off, as B16/2 No. 61435 runs round the second portion of the seven-coach train. The reason for splitting for this manoeuvre was that the track immediately beyond the station was too poor to handle the whole rake in one go.

Most of the tour participants appear to be out of the train – no doubt glad to stretch their legs after a two hour trip from Northallerton! – either watching and waiting or casually strolling around the station, perhaps aware that they will probably not be here again. Note the attractive design of this wayside station.

Right **BOROUGHBRIDGE** An earlier part of the tour had seen ex-LMS 'Black 5' 4-6-0 No. 44790 haul the train from Harrogate to Boroughbridge and on to Starbeck. It is seen at Boroughbridge Goods, where there are problems!

A late strengthening of the train to seven coaches prevented the loco running round, leading to the train having to reverse. Never a satisfactory situation, it was made worse by poor rail conditions and a sharp curve on an adverse gradient! Here, the fireman and a tour participant (possibly one of the organisers?) appear to be having some discussion over the position, with other tour members looking on.

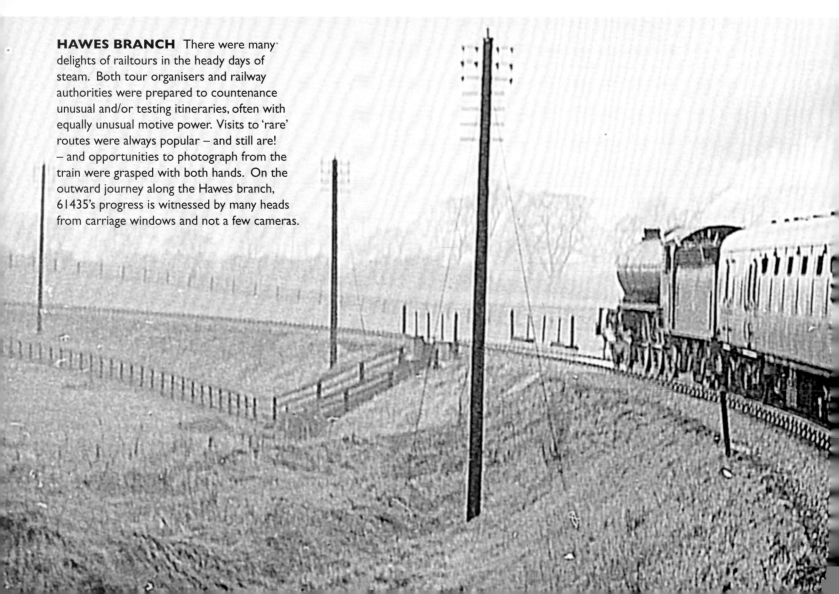

HAWES BRANCH There were many
delights of railtours in the heady days of
steam. Both tour organisers and railway
authorities were prepared to countenance
unusual and/or testing itineraries, often with
equally unusual motive power. Visits to 'rare'
routes were always popular – and still are!
– and opportunities to photograph from the
train were grasped with both hands. On the
outward journey along the Hawes branch,
61435's progress is witnessed by many heads
from carriage windows and not a few cameras.

NORTHALLERTON Having safely negotiated the return from Hawes – taking nearly two hours – the tour now has another change of motive power. At Castle Hills Inner Junction, near Northallerton, ex-LMS Stanier '4' 2-6-4T No 42639 and ex-LNER Class V3 No. 67646 are back-to-back as they head towards the photographer and the train. Departure from here was booked for around 3.45 p.m. but it is unknown how late they were when photographed! More ties and suits are in evidence – and, obviously, the rain has stopped – and there is even a token female present!

For our final views of railtours we return to two already visited.

One month later the RCTS ran another railtour, this time a little further south. The 'North Staffordshire Rail Tour' of 30 May saw another ex-LMS 'Black 5' on duty, for the whole tour on this occasion. Leaving Birmingham (Snow Hill) at 10.30 a.m., the six coach special first headed west along ex-GWR tracks into Shropshire (to Wellington and Market Drayton) before moving northeast into Staffordshire.

Most of the erstwhile North Staffs. Railway lines and branches were covered before a return to Birmingham via the ex-LNWR route through Rugeley (Trent Valley). As seen at this unidentified location, 45020 was in immaculate condition, having just returned from overhaul at Cowlairs Works, Glasgow. Note that shirt sleeves – still with ties, however! – were more the order of the day.

Platform end consternation! As already seen on p.14, the M7 locomotive booked to relieve Q1 No. 33035 on 'The Hampshire Hog' tour of 14 March failed and this is no doubt what is the focus of debate here in the pouring rain. The driver waits patiently for instructions, with the road clear ahead as evidenced by the semaphore signal, while the rest of the assembled group deliberate. Note the progression of hierarchy, judged by working clothes to greatcoat and caps to bowler! ? Another interested party shelters from the rain inside the front coach!

Left **CHRIST'S HOSPITAL** Exchanging the token. A pleasant enough job in shirt sleeve conditions, but not so enjoyable at other times. In the late afternoon of an unidentified summer's day, an equally unidentified 'Mickey Mouse' Ivatt '2' 2-6-2T slides into Christ's Hospital station. The signalman prepares to hand the baton to the fireman, to give him authority to proceed onto and along the branch to Peasmarsh Junction and Guildford. Without this official token in his hand, the driver cannot continue, as without it there could be a danger of collision on the single track branch.

Right **READING** We have seen a 'Standard 4' 2-6-4T before (see p.21) and a later example is seen here in the guise of No. 80140, one of the last few built out of a class of 155. First introduced in 1951, following Nationalisation of the railways in 1948, they were truly 'maids of all work' and could be seen throughout the country undertaking all manner of passenger and freight duties, other than the top link jobs. Here, photographed from the neighbouring embankment by the ex-GWR main line out of Paddington, No. 80140 pauses for a replenishment of coal supplies at Reading (South) shed on 4 March. Note the looming presence of some of Reading's business emporia in the background.

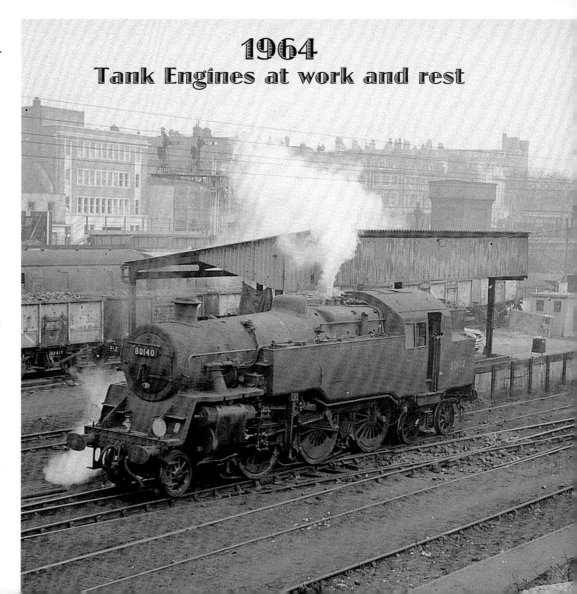

1964
Tank Engines at work and rest

Below **GUILDFORD** Yet another 'Mickey Mouse' and yet another turn of duty for a class member. No. 41287 briefly pauses in Guildford station on 31 July, while hauling a defective EMU, 2-BIL No.2093, from Platform 8 to the nearby sidings. To the right are the entrance roads to the shed and above the footbridge from which the photograph on p.12 was taken. A pre-war design, the 2-BIL fleet was nearing the end at this time. By contrast, 41287 was a relative 'spring chicken', being new to traffic in December 1950, to Crewe North shed. After several reallocations, the move to the SR came, with others of the class, in 1961. Initially to Brighton, it moved to Guildford shed two months prior to this view. A subsequent move to Basingstoke in 1965 ended with withdrawal on 22 August 1966.

1964
Happenings (4)

JULY

- Serious escalation in the Vietnam War as US death toll passes 400
- US sends 5000 more troops to Vietnam bringing the total deployed to 21,000
- Malawi declares Independence from Britain
- **Wimbledon**
  Roy Emerson beats Fred Stolle to win Men's Singles Final:
  6-4, 12-10, 4-6, 6-3
  Maria Bueno beats Margaret Smith to win Women's Singles Final:
  6-4, 7-9 6-3
- **Donald Campbell**
  sets record for turbine vehicle, 690.91 kph (429.31 mph)

AUGUST

- Viet Cong gunboats attack US Destroyers in Gulf of Tonkin
- Last hanging takes place in Britain

Above **GUILDFORD** If you thought that this tank locomotive does not look like a normal British type, you would be correct. Initially built from 1942 for the U S Army Transportation Corps, a few became 'surplus to requirements' with the end of hostilities and the SR bought fourteen in 1946. Weighing a relatively light 46 tons 10 cwt, they were able to work in restricted areas and Southampton Docks had a number, including 30064, seen here on Guildford shed. With the closure of the shed on the Docks in 1963, '64' moved initially to Eastleigh shed before a further move, to Basingstoke in November 1966. The end came at that depot eight months later, only days before the end of steam on the SR.

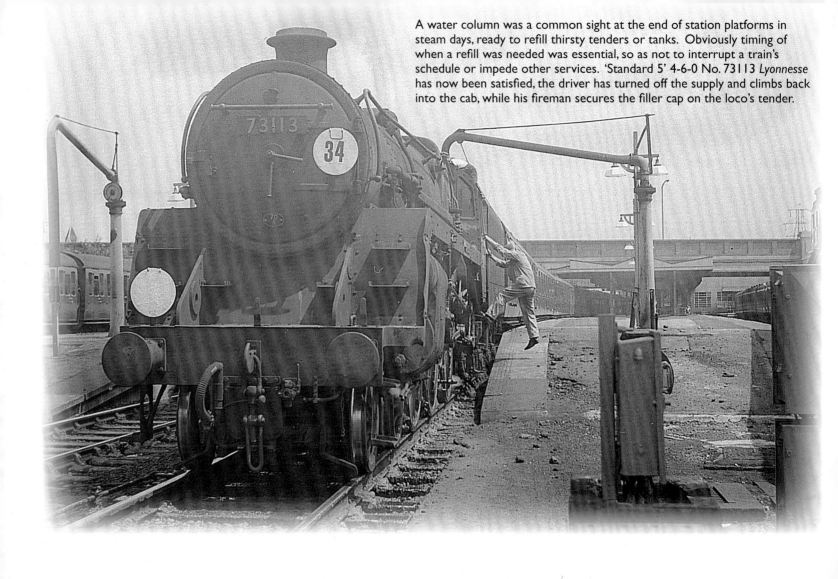

A water column was a common sight at the end of station platforms in steam days, ready to refill thirsty tenders or tanks. Obviously timing of when a refill was needed was essential, so as not to interrupt a train's schedule or impede other services. 'Standard 5' 4-6-0 No. 73113 *Lyonnesse* has now been satisfied, the driver has turned off the supply and climbs back into the cab, while his fireman secures the filler cap on the loco's tender.

1964
Thirsty work!

GUILDFORD Tank engines could be just as thirsty as tender variants, indeed on occasions more so, as their tanks potentially had less capacity. At Guildford on 8 March, 'Standard 4' 2-6-4T No. 80032 is in the process of having a long drink, carefully watched over by the fireman. Note the rather unique, 'low slung' column design on this platform.

Right **READING** Yet another unusual design is captured for posterity at the end of Reading (Southern) station platform on 13 March. An old SER design, it was highly unusual to find a double-sided column with wheels attached to the column side.

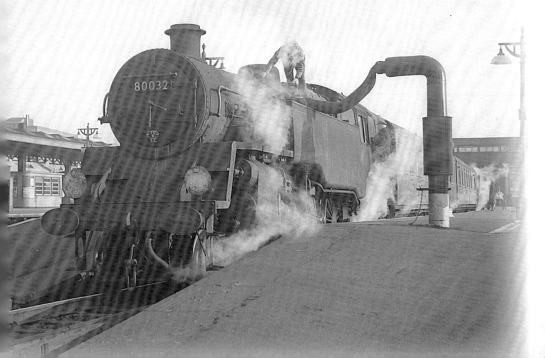

A brief view inside the cab of a steam loco shows a fireman operating instruments on his side of the footplate. Again, the variety and complexity of the cab controls are demonstrated, along with the Advance Warning System dial, top left.

1964
No 1 Records

January

I want to hold your hand	The Beatles
Glad all over	The Dave Clark Five
Needles & Pins	The Searchers

February

| Diane | The Bachelors |
| Anyone who had a heart | Cilla Black |

March

| Little children | Billy J. Kramer & The Dakotas |

April

| Can't buy me love | The Beatles |
| A world without love | Peter & Gordon |

May

Don't throw your love away	The Searchers
Juliet	The Four Pennies
You're my world	Cilla Black

June

| It's over | Roy Orbison |

July

The house of the rising sun	The Animals
It's all over now	The Rolling Stones
A hard days night	The Beatles

August

| Doo wah diddy diddy | Manfred Mann |
| Have I the right? | The Honeycombs |

September

| You really got me | The Kinks |
| I'm into something good | Herman's Hermits |

October

| Oh pretty woman | Roy Orbison |
| Always something there to remind me | Sandie Shaw |

November

| Baby love | The Supremes |

December

| Little red rooster | The Rolling Stones |
| I feel fine | The Beatles |

SALISBURY A more standard arrangement of water column is that seen here at Salisbury station on 12 May. This time the driver watches the ingress of water to the tank, while his fireman receives assistance with moving the supply of coal towards the front of the tender, for easier access during the journey. The upturned 'thimble' on the platform by the column was to catch any still gushing water from the pipe after use. 'Merchant Navy' 35024 *East Asiatic Company* will no doubt benefit from the refill when it restarts its journey as the westbound 'Atlantic Coast Express'.

READING How the mighty are fallen! No matter how well a machine is maintained, there can be failures. On the railway this can be extremely inconvenient if the power hauling a train ceases to function properly and one way to overcome this in steam days was to have a spare locomotive ready to act at a moment's notice. Referred to as 'station pilot', it also had the benefit of being available for fill-in duties as well, but when the level of type used is as here – an ex-front line express loco – it does seem a waste of a valuable asset. However, 'Castle' Class No.4089 *Donnington Castle*, seen in this role on 14 April at the side of Reading (General) station, had seen better days. Allocated to Reading shed on 28 December 1963, it is here without front numberplate and original cabside numbers and would only continue active service for a further six months.

CROWTHORNE The early 1960s saw increasing numbers of new diesels of all types introduced onto our railways, with even greater numbers of steam being replaced and sent to the scrap yards. Cross country services were some of the earliest in turning over to dieselisation and an example here sees 'Hymek' D7027 (built by Beyer Peacock in Manchester in April 1962) at speed between Crowthorne and Sandhurst, operating a Wolverhampton-North Camp special for the Farnborough Air Display of a sunny 13 September. Admittedly a special working, but note the eleven coaches allocated to impending travellers

1964
Out and about
roaming the rails

1964
Happenings (5)

FARNBOROUGH Despite the comments on p.45, steam did cling on in parts of the UK and the meandering, indirect and non-main line route from Reading to Redhill was one such area. On 20 August, '4300' Class 2-6-0 No. 6309 is not under any undue strain as it leaves Farnborough North station with the four-coach 6.50 p.m. Reading (Southern)-Redhill stopping service. Despite looking in good order, however, the loco was withdrawn from service just six weeks later, on 12 October.

SEPTEMBER

- Forth Road Bridge opens to traffic
- The Sun newspaper launched in place of the Daily Herald
- Malta gains Independence from Britain

OCTOBER

- Olympic Games held in Tokyo
- Krushchev replaced as Russian premier by Brezhnev and Kosygin
- Labour win General Election ending 13 years of Tory rule - Harold Wilson PM

NOVEMBER

- Death Penalty abolished by UK Government

DECEMBER

- UK Government announces that *Dr Richard Beeching* is to leave British Railways. During his almost 4 year tenure many thousands of route miles and hundreds of staions were closed - a policy of much debate ever since

LYMINGTON PIER At various points around the UK coastline, railways and ferries met, providing complementary services to each other. The very short ex-L&SWR branch from Brockenhurst to Lymington Pier provided a vital service for both locals on this part of the mainland and, also, for traffic to and from the Isle of Wight via Yarmouth. On 4 August, yet another 'Mickey Mouse' 2-6-2T, No. 41270, stands at the Pier station waiting for the road to be the 5.25 p.m. departure, having collected passengers and some small items of freight from the ferry tied up alongside. General freight services were withdrawn from the branch on 9 August 1965, but, happily, passenger facilities survive to this day, operated by the only remaining slam-door electric multiple units in the country.

Index

Acknowledgements

As with projects of any size and/or complexity, there are many people 'behind the scenes' who give of their time, expertise, advice, etc. willingly but often receive little in the way of thanks in return. The same is true with this new series, with the exception that the team putting the launch titles together has been smaller than is the norm.

There have been others 'in the wings', but the core personalities who deserve especial mention – apart from the two authors, whose patience, tolerance and friendship have somehow survived long hours, tight deadlines and frustration with some lack of information from the original photographs (!) – are Brian Morrison, for his constant and ever-ready willingness to offer assistance, advice and research facilities and for proof reading so quickly; and Sharon Rich, for her common sense approach and comments. This is her first excursion into the world of publishing and not only has it been eye-opener for her, but she has added a vital ingredient of not being an existing railway enthusiast! She has also coped remarkably well with those same tight deadlines, on top of managing her family and domestic duties!

Paul Shannon and John Vaughan deserve mention for specialist information on specific pictures.

Peter Rowlands is also thanked for his early enthusiasm, encouragement and for helping to drum up outside support; and Connie Ruffell for permission to use one or two specific photographs. Frances Townsend for sustaining her husband through the process! Without these individuals, the project would not have achieved what it already has.